TWO-DOLLAR BILLS

BY MADDIE SPALDING

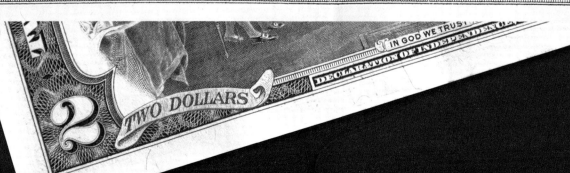

The Child's World®
childsworld.com

Published by The Child's World®
1980 Lookout Drive • Mankato, MN 56003-1705
800-599-READ • www.childsworld.com

ISBN 9781503820081
LCCN 2016960505

Printed in the United States of America
PA02336

ABOUT THE AUTHOR

Maddie Spalding writes and
edits children's books. She lives in
Minnesota.

TABLE OF CONTENTS

CHAPTER ONE

WHAT IS A TWO-DOLLAR BILL?

Two-dollar bills are a type of money. Two one-dollar bills equal one two-dollar bill. The Bureau of Engraving and Printing (BEP) makes two-dollar bills. Bills are made from cotton and **linen**.

Two one-dollar bills equal one two-dollar bill.

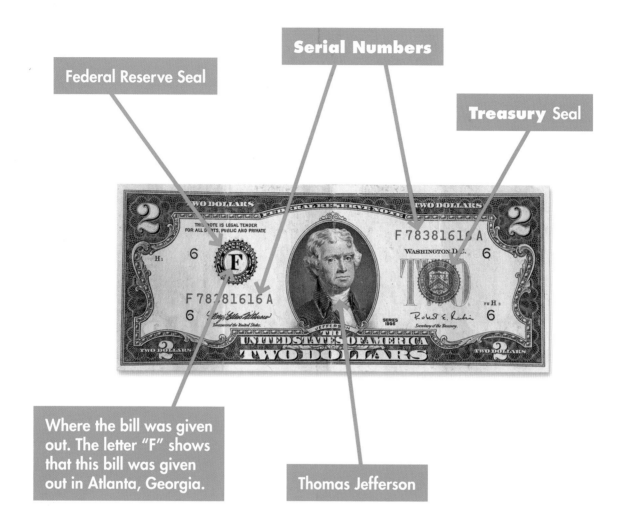

Federal Reserve Seal

Serial Numbers

Treasury Seal

Where the bill was given out. The letter "F" shows that this bill was given out in Atlanta, Georgia.

Thomas Jefferson

Former president Thomas Jefferson is on the front of the two-dollar bill.

Why do you think the signing of the Declaration of Independence appears on the back of the two-dollar bill?

Thomas Jefferson

Benjamin Franklin

Declaration of Independence

John Hancock

The back of the bill shows the signing of the Declaration of Independence.

CHAPTER TWO

SECURITY FEATURES

Two-dollar bills have serial numbers. Each two-dollar bill has a different serial number.

Serial numbers help banks identify bills.

The U.S. Department of the Treasury was created in 1789.

There are two **seals** on the two-dollar bill. One is the U.S. Department of the Treasury seal.

Another seal shows the Federal Reserve Bank that gave out the bill. These details make it more difficult for people to make fake bills.

There are 12 Federal Reserve Banks across the country. Why do you think this is true?

One bank that gives out bills is in Boston, Massachusetts.

CHAPTER THREE

THE HISTORY OF THE TWO-DOLLAR BILL

The first U.S. two-dollar bills were made in 1862. Alexander Hamilton was on the front. He was one of the Founding Fathers of the United States.

Alexander Hamilton was the first secretary of the U.S. Treasury (1789–1795).

Thomas Jefferson was put on the front of the two-dollar bill in 1869. Jefferson's house was put on the back of the bill in 1928.

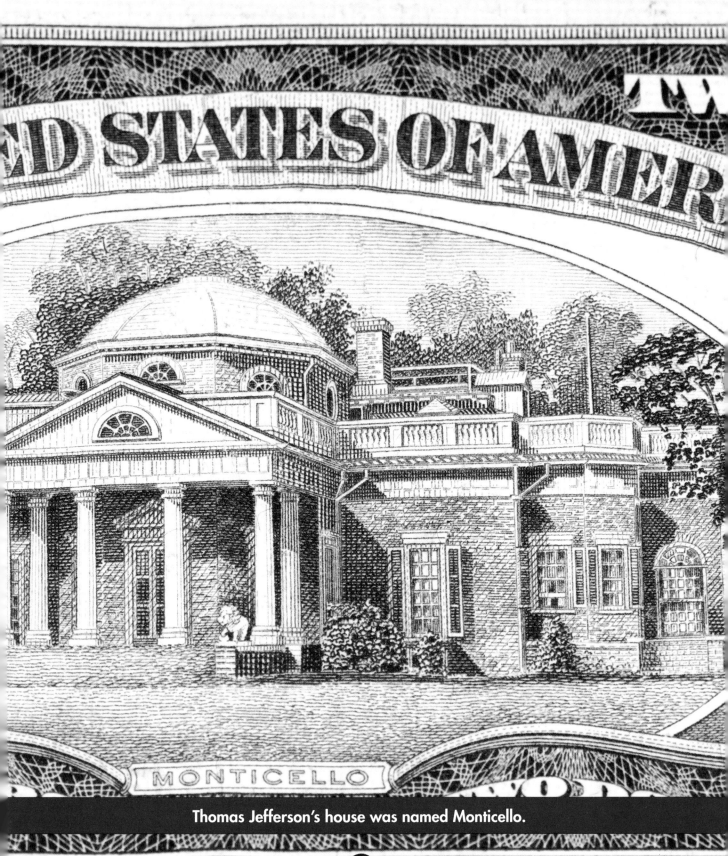

Thomas Jefferson's house was named Monticello.

A new image was put on the back of the bill in 1976. It celebrated the 200 years since the founding of the United States. It showed the signing of the Declaration of Independence.

How are the images on the front and back of the two-dollar bill related?

THOMAS JEFFERSON was

the third president of the United States
(1801–1809). He wrote the Declaration of
Independence.

1869 U.S. two-dollar bill

 1862 The first U.S. two-dollar bills were made.

 1869 Thomas Jefferson was put on the front of the two-dollar bill.

1928 Jefferson's house was put on the back of the two-dollar bill.

Back of the 1953 U.S. two-dollar bill

 1976 The image on the back of the two-dollar bill changed. The new image showed the signing of the Declaration of Independence.

Back of the 1976 U.S. two-dollar bill

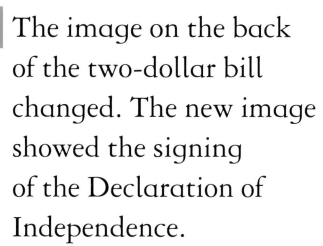

★ The image on the back of the current two-dollar bill is based on a painting by artist John Trumbull.

★ There were 47 men in Trumbull's painting. But there are only 42 men on the back of the two-dollar bill. There was not enough space to include all 47 men.

★ The BEP makes just over one billion two-dollar bills each year.

★ The BEP stopped making two-dollar bills in 1966. People were not spending them. The BEP began making two-dollar bills again in 1976.

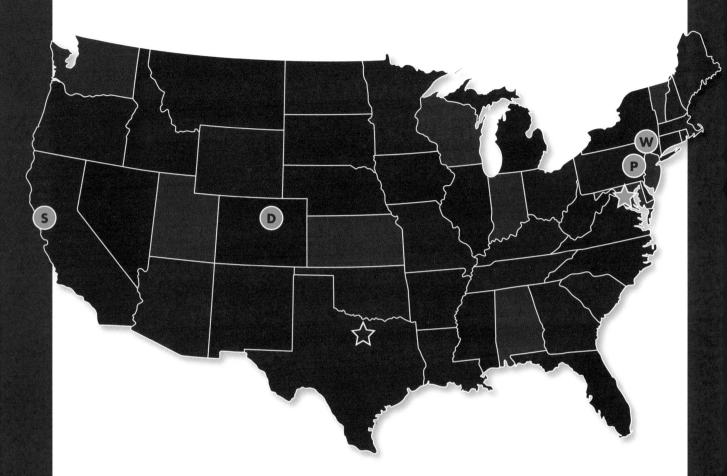

BUREAU OF ENGRAVING AND PRINTING OFFICES

★ Fort Worth, Texas

★ Washington, DC

COIN-PRODUCING MINTS

D Denver, Colorado—Produces coins marked with a D.

P Philadelphia, Pennsylvania—Produces coins marked with a P.

S San Francisco, California—Produces coins marked with an S.

W West Point, New York—Produces coins marked with a W.

linen (LIN-uhn) Linen is a strong type of cloth. Two-dollar bills are made from cotton and linen.

seals (SEELS) Seals are images that are used on official government documents. There are two seals on the two-dollar bill.

serial numbers (SEER-ee-ull NUM-burz) Serial numbers are numbers that identify something. Two-dollar bills have serial numbers.

Treasury (TREZH-ur-ee) A Treasury is a part of a government that is in charge of a country's money. The U.S. Department of the Treasury is in charge of money in the United States.

IN THE LIBRARY

Gregory, Josh. *Thomas Jefferson: The 3rd President.*
New York, NY: Bearport, 2015.

Jozefowicz, Chris. *10 Fascinating Facts about Dollar Bills.*
New York, NY: Children's Press, 2016.

Schuh, Mari C. *Counting Money.* Minneapolis, MN:
Bellwether, 2016.

ON THE WEB

Visit our Web site for links about
two-dollar bills: childsworld.com/links

Note to Parents, Teachers, and Librarians: We routinely verify our Web links to make sure
they are safe and active sites. So encourage your readers to check them out!

INDEX